21st CENTURY SAXOPHONE SERIES

SUMMER TRIANGLE
Yukiko Nishimura

for Alto Saxophone and Piano

PIANO

Commissioned and Premiered by Masato Kumoi

keisersouthernmusic.com

PROGRAM NOTE

Well-known Japanese saxophonist, Masato Kumoi, commissioned this work after hearing composer Yukiko Nishimura's popular band work, *Star Ship*. His request was for a new solo alto saxophone and band piece that included the same main theme. The composer drew inspiration for *Summer Triangle* from familiar astronomical geometry; "an imaginary triangle drawn on the northern hemisphere's celestial sphere, with its defining vertices at Altair, Deneb and Vega, the brightest stars in the three constellations of Aquila, Cygnus and Lyra, respectively." The movement titles represent each of these stars: 1. *Aquila*, 2. *Lyra (Star Ship)* and 3. *Cygnus*.

PERFORMANCE NOTES

Movement 1 : Keep the tension of all melody lines by connecting long and short notes.
Movement 2 : Enjoy the conversation between the saxophone solo and band.
Movement 3 : Even when the melody is lively, make sure to keep a relaxed feeling. Enjoy the sweet and smooth atmosphere from "Q" to "S."

ABOUT THE COMPOSER

Composer and pianist, **Yukiko Nishimura**, grew up in Japan. Ms. Nishimura graduated from Tokyo National University of Arts in 1990, where she studied with Atsutada Otaka. In 1991, she moved to Florida to study with Dr. Alfred Reed at the University of Miami and in 1993, she continued her studies with Dr. Richard Danielpour at Manhattan School of Music. Other notable teachers include Ivan Davis, Dr. Sara Davis Buechner and Giampaolo Bracali.

As a composer, Ms. Nishimura has received numerous commissions and has written for many solo instruments, chamber groups, wind ensemble, strings, and full orchestra. She has composed the scores to several notable silent films in America and Japan, such as Edison's **1910 Frankenstein**, and **The Water Magician**, directed by Kenji Mizoguchi, as well as collaborated with Noh Play, Japanese traditional theaters. Among her honors are the special mention at the 15th and 26th International Competition for Original Compositions for Band in Corciano, Italy, and the 6th Aoyama Award.

Ms. Nishimura is an active pianist that has given many solo concerts around the world, from Japan to the New York Public Library.

Summer Triangle

for alto saxophone and piano

I. Aguila

Yukiko Nishimura

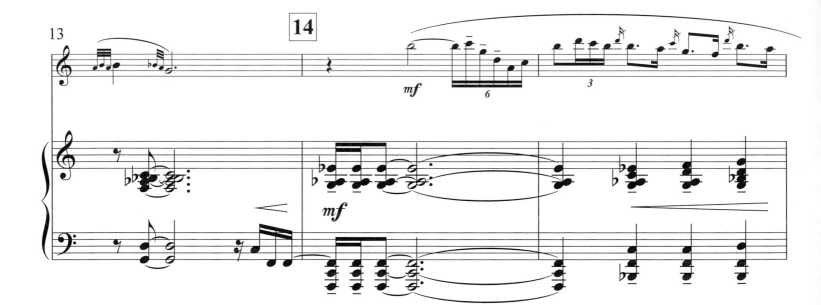

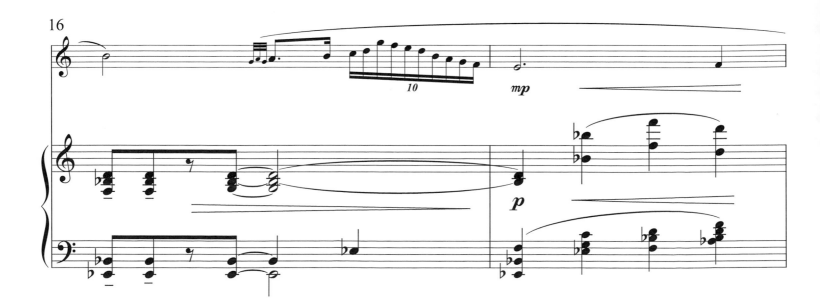

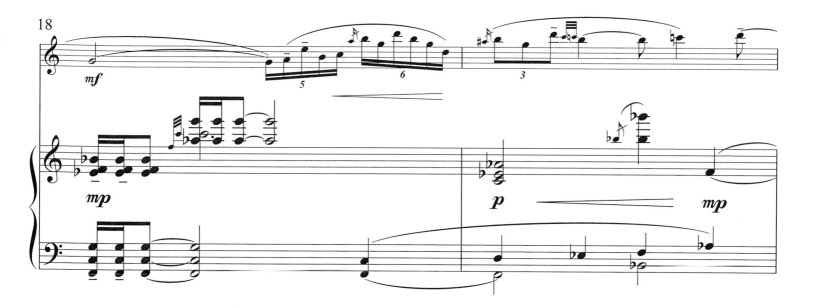

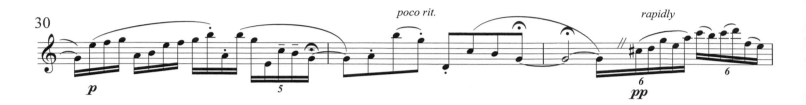

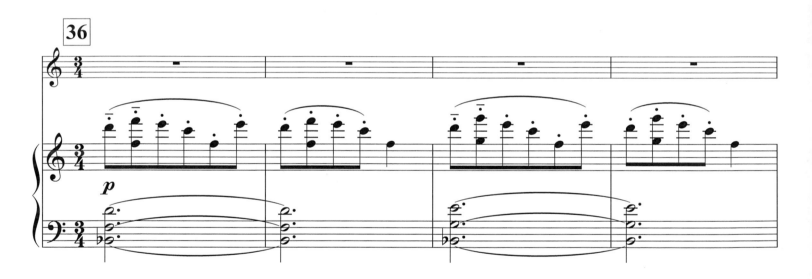

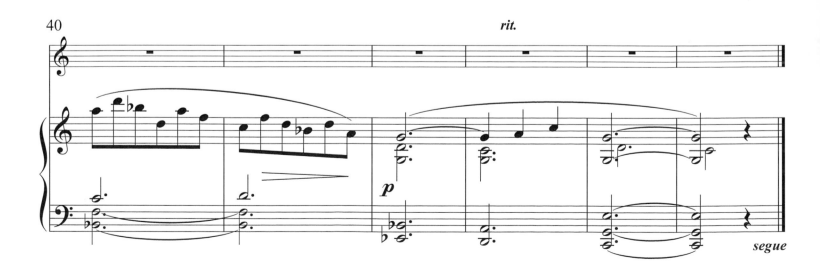

II. Lyra (Star Ship)

27

31

37 *sentimentally*

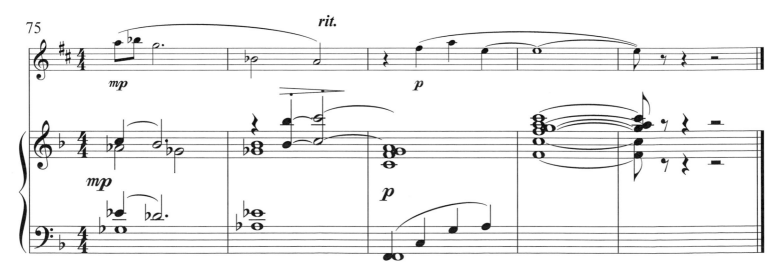

III. Cygnus

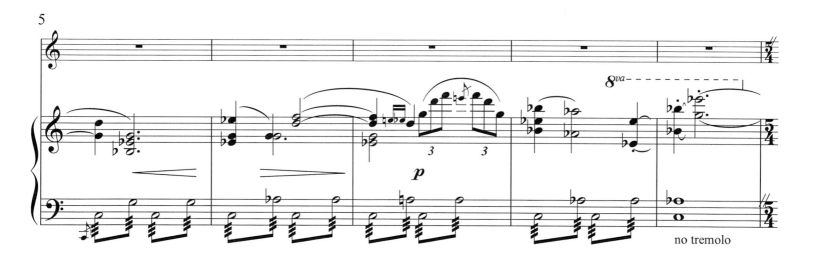

21st CENTURY SAXOPHONE SERIES

SUMMER TRIANGLE
Yukiko Nishimura

for Alto Saxophone and Piano

ALTO SAXOPHONE

Commissioned and Premiered by Masato Kumoi

keisersouthernmusic.com

PROGRAM NOTE

Well-known Japanese saxophonist, Masato Kumoi, commissioned this work after hearing composer Yukiko Nishimura's popular band work, *Star Ship*. His request was for a new solo alto saxophone and band piece that included the same main theme. The composer drew inspiration for *Summer Triangle* from familiar astronomical geometry; "an imaginary triangle drawn on the northern hemisphere's celestial sphere, with its defining vertices at Altair, Deneb and Vega, the brightest stars in the three constellations of Aquila, Cygnus and Lyra, respectively." The movement titles represent each of these stars: 1. *Aquila*, 2. *Lyra (Star Ship)* and 3. *Cygnus*.

PERFORMANCE NOTES

Movement 1 : Keep the tension of all melody lines by connecting long and short notes.
Movement 2 : Enjoy the conversation between the saxophone solo and band.
Movement 3 : Even when the melody is lively, make sure to keep a relaxed feeling. Enjoy the sweet and smooth atmosphere from "Q" to "S."

ABOUT THE COMPOSER

Composer and pianist, **Yukiko Nishimura**, grew up in Japan. Ms. Nishimura graduated from Tokyo National University of Arts in 1990, where she studied with Atsutada Otaka. In 1991, she moved to Florida to study with Dr. Alfred Reed at the University of Miami and in 1993, she continued her studies with Dr. Richard Danielpour at Manhattan School of Music. Other notable teachers include Ivan Davis, Dr. Sara Davis Buechner and Giampaolo Bracali.

As a composer, Ms. Nishimura has received numerous commissions and has written for many solo instruments, chamber groups, wind ensemble, strings, and full orchestra. She has composed the scores to several notable silent films in America and Japan, such as Edison's **1910 Frankenstein**, and **The Water Magician**, directed by Kenji Mizoguchi, as well as collaborated with Noh Play, Japanese traditional theaters. Among her honors are the special mention at the 15th and 26th International Competition for Original Compositions for Band in Corciano, Italy, and the 6th Aoyama Award.

Ms. Nishimura is an active pianist that has given many solo concerts around the world, from Japan to the New York Public Library.

Summer Triangle

for alto saxophone and piano

Yukiko Nishimura

I. Aguila

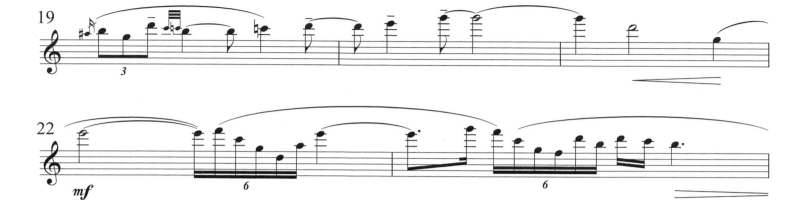

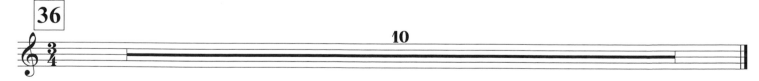

4

II. Lyra (Star Ship)

III. Cygnus

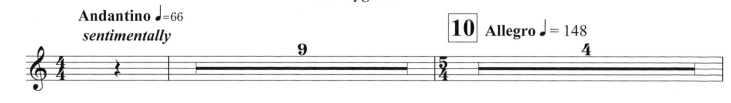

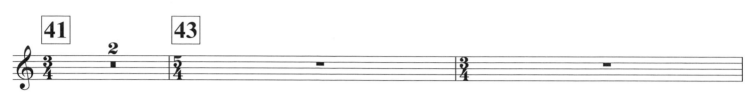

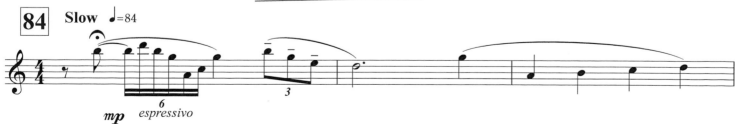

molto rit.

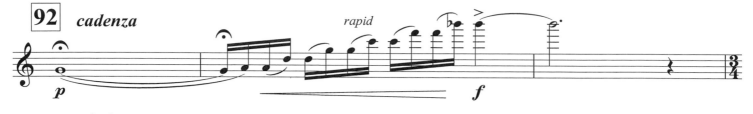

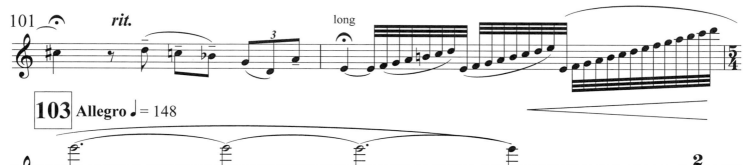

3

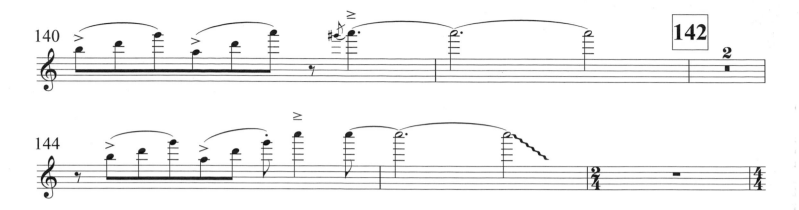

57 **Meno mosso** ♩=128

60

63

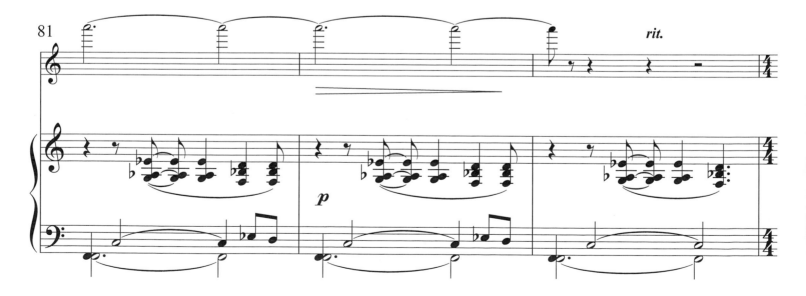

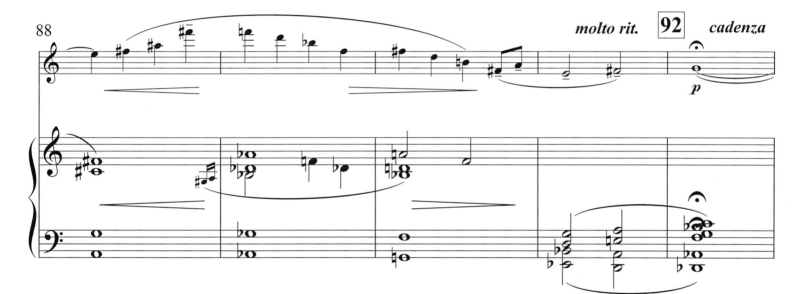

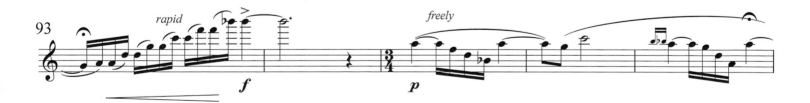

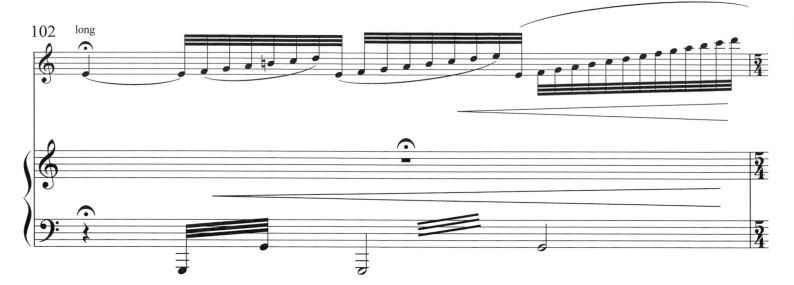

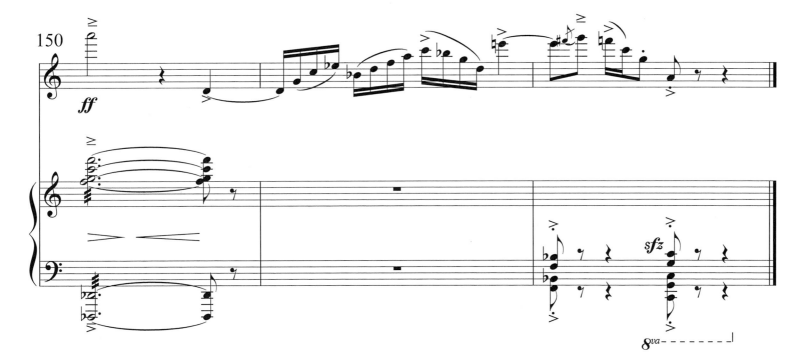

Selected Alto Saxophone Publications

SOLO WITH PIANO

BOZZA, EUGENE
Hite, David

SS193 Divertissement (Grade 4) 3773803

This edition of Eugene Bozza's Divertissement, Op 39, can be performed on either baritone or alto saxophone. The work is in a single movement, encompassing sections of varying tempi, keys and styles. It is ideally suited for the clarinet and saxophone as are Bozza's Fantasie Italienne and Aria which are published for both of these instruments.

DEMERSSEMAN, JULES
Hemke, Fred

ST520 Carnival of Venice (Grade 4) 3775239

Carnival of Venice was originally written for saxophonist Adolphe Mayeur, who was a student of Adolphe Sax, the inventor of the instrument. A band arrangement by Herbert Clarke and R. Mark Rogers that uses Fred Hemke's solo part is also available from the

HANDEL, GEORGE FRIDERIC
Gee, Harry

SS749 Adagio and Allegro (Grade 2) 3774410

This solo piece, originally written for oboe and continuo in C minor, includes the 1st and 2nd movements of Handel's Sonata No. 1., Op. 1, No. 8, HWV 366.

HAYDN, FRANZ JOSEPH
Voxman, Himie/ Block, R.P.

ST758 Adagio Cantabile and Presto (Grade 2) 3775566

HAYDN, FRANZ JOSEPH
Wienandt, Elwyn

SS542 Serenade (Grade 3) 3774180

This serenade from Haydn's String Quartet Op. 3, No. 5 (Andante Cantabile) is a beautifully lyrical selection for the intermediate player. Arrangements by Elwyn Wienandt are available from the publisher for both clarinet and alto saxophone.

KOCH, FREDERICK

SU112 Three Latin Moods (Grade 3) 3775931

KREISLER, ALEXANDER VON

SS525 Two Impressions (Grade 4) 3774159

This two-movement impressionist piece by Russian composer Alexander von Kreisler contains a legato, dream-like Andante section followed by an articulate and frantic Allegro section. These contrasting movements make this piece a perfect fit for juries, contests, and recitals. Movements: I. Andante II. Allegro

LACOMBE, PAUL
Andraud, Albert J.

ST236 Rigaudon for Alto Saxophone and Piano (Grade 4) 3774850

Versions for Clarinet in Bb, Alto Clarinet in Eb, Alto Saxophone, and Tenor Saxophone are available from the publisher.

LOEILLET, JEAN BAPTISTE
Merriman, Lyle

SS886 Sonata (Grade 3) 3774563

This two movement (slow-fast) sonata gives the intermediate player the opportunity to practice both lyrical and technical playing. It is a great selection for both contest or recital.

LUNDE, LAWSON

SS743 Sonata for Alto Saxophone (Grade 5) 3774405

A very versatile piece for alto saxophone, this work is recognizably American in quality, and is filled with energy, lovely melodies, and some jazz harmonies.

MORITZ, EDVARD
Leeson, Cecil

SS794 Sonata, Op. 96 for Alto Saxophone (Grade 4) 3774461

This four movment sonata combines beautiful lyrical writing with interspersed segments of technical flair. It is a wonderful recital selection for the advancing player, either in total or just individual movements. It is dedicated to Cecil Leeson.

PIERNE, GABRIEL
Gee, Harry

ST48 Canzonetta (Grade 5) 3775178

Originally written for clarinet and piano, this canzonetta by Pierne has been transcribed for either Eb alto saxophone, Bb tenor saxophone or soprano saxophone.

REED, ALFRED

SS764 Ballade (Grade 3) 3774427

Written for Vincent J. "Jimmy" Abato, a brilliant virtuoso both on the clarinet and saxophone. An accompaniment for concert band is also available from Southern Music.

RIMSKY-KORSAKOV, NICOLAI
Leeson, Cecil

ST439 Flight of the Bumblebee (Grade 5) 3775125

This transcription for alto saxophone is dedicated to Arthur C. Fernald.

SCHUDEL, THOMAS

SU288 Intrada (Grade 2) 3776168

This piece is a wonderful early intermediate selection for contest or recital.

SCHUMANN, ROBERT
Hemke, Fred

ST38 Three Romances, Op. 94 (Grade 5) 3775044

"as your bride, you must indeed dedicate something further to me, and I know of nothing more tender than these 3 Romances, in particular the middle one, which is the most beautiful love duet." Despite these words by Clara Schumann, her husband did not consider his 1849 Christmas gift of these three romances to be "good or worthy enough" of her. All the same, these romances, originally written for oboe and piano, became one of Schumann's most successful compositions.

SENAILLE, JEAN BAPTISTE
Gee, Harry

SS501 Allegro Spiritoso (Grade 4) 3774134

The "Allegro Spiritoso" is the 3rd movement of a Sonata in D Minor. Versions for following instruments are available from the publisher: alto clarinet, bass clarinet, contra alto clarinet, contrabass clarinet, alto saxophone, tenor saxophone, baritone saxophone, bassoon, euphonium/trombone, and tuba.

TUTHILL, BURNET

SS497 Sonata for Alto Saxophone, Op. 20 (Grade 5) 3774129

This is a three movement sonata that is published in the Contemporary Saxophone Series.

WALTERS, DAVID

SS901 Episode (Grade 2) 3774584

The composer graduated from the U.S. Naval School of Music during World War II and ultimately became director of orchestra and band at Jacksonville State University.

WARD, DAVID

SS101 An Abstract (Grade 3) 3773701

This piece is a wonderful introduction to atonal music for the intermediate player.

WEINBERGER, JAROMIR
Willems, Tristan

SU821 Alto Saxophone Concerto (solo/ piano reduction) (Grade 5) 298123

Jaromir Weinberger, a noted Czech composer, achieved sudden fame in 1927 with the production of his opera, Svanda dudâk (Schwanda, the Bagpiper), written in a popular Bohemian style, at the Czech Opera in Prague. Weinberger fled Europe under the growing Nazi threat and took up residence in New York in 1939, where he enjoyed a number of major orchestral performances and commissions of all kinds. One of these came from renowned saxophonist Cecil Leeson, who asked Weinberger to compose a concerto for alto saxophone and orchestra.

Due to the outbreak of World War II, the premiere would not happen until 1946, six years after the completion of the concerto in piano score. The work was revised following the premiere, and it is only now that those revisions have been incorporated into the solo saxophone and piano reduction with this performance edition by Weinberger scholar, publisher and saxophonist Tristan Willems.

YOUNG, CHARLES ROCHESTER

SU507 Concerto for Alto Saxophone and Wind Ensemble 3776428

Well-known Japanese saxophonist, Masato Kumoi, commissioned this work after hearing composer Yukiko Nishimura's popular band work, *Star Ship*. His request was for a new solo alto saxophone and band piece that included the same main theme. The composer drew inspiration for *Summer Triangle* from familiar astronomical geometry; "an imaginary triangle drawn on the northern hemisphere's celestial sphere, with its defining vertices at Altair, Deneb and Vega, the brightest stars in the three constellations of Aquila, Cygnus and Lyra, respectively." The movement titles represent each of these stars:
1. *Aquila*, 2. *Lyra (Star Ship)* and 3. *Cygnus*.

ABOUT THE COMPOSER

Composer and pianist, **Yukiko Nishimura**, grew up in Japan. Ms. Nishimura graduated from Tokyo National University of Arts in 1990, where she studied with Atsutada Otaka. In 1991, she moved to Florida to study with Dr. Alfred Reed at the University of Miami and in 1993, she continued her studies with Dr. Richard Danielpour at Manhattan School of Music. Other notable teachers include Ivan Davis, Dr. Sara Davis Buechner and Giampaolo Bracali.

As a composer, Ms. Nishimura has received numerous commissions and has written for many solo instruments, chamber groups, wind ensemble, strings, and full orchestra. She has composed the scores to several notable silent films in America and Japan, such as Edison's **1910 Frankenstein**, and **The Water Magician**, directed by Kenji Mizoguchi, as well as collaborated with Noh Play, Japanese traditional theaters. Among her honors are the special mention at the 15th and 26th International Competition for Original Compositions for Band in Corciano, Italy, and the 6th Aoyama Award.

Ms. Nishimura is an active pianist that has given many solo concerts around the world, from Japan to the New York Public Library.

EXCLUSIVELY DISTRIBUTED BY
HAL•LEONARD®

EAN 13

9 781581 066203

keisersouthernmusic.com

U.S. $19.95

8 88680 95090 3

SU799
HL00298121